Four Mile

poems by

Paul Stroble

Finishing Line Press
Georgetown, Kentucky

Four Mile

Publisher: Leah Huete de Maines

Editor: Christen Kincaid

Cover Art: Paul Stroble

Author Photo: Beth Stroble

Cover Design: Elizabeth Maines McCleavy

Order online: www.finishinglinepress.com
also available on amazon.com

Author inquiries and mail orders:
Finishing Line Press
P. O. Box 1626
Georgetown, Kentucky 40324
U. S. A.

Table of Contents

I

Homesick

*

How beautiful a highway
          near my hometown,
     four miles of Illinois prairie
where I'd be proud to have my cremains
cast along the right of way,

ashes and ashes
          upon day lilies, Queen Anne's lace
and switchgrass
in the highway ditch hosting
          yesterday's rain.

          Daffodils
may be psalms, foolish and bold
          as fortune.
But my psalms start at Four Mile,
all the farmhouses and neighbors,
familiar fields,
the country church,
          the family graveyard:
                    the way to Grandma's.

I drive out here
          whenever I can.

Pencil measurements
of my soul were sketched
          on wood frames

and God knit
          the cloths of myself
that flip in the wind on country clotheslines.

*

Sheltering
for these weeks

I travel my hands' secret heartline:

Route 185,
up the slight hill
        past the young girl's grave;
the road's gray, humble width
        laid in 1920s specs,
and then a few minutes' drive

until I reach the curve into timber
past the Brownstown Road
        and this prairie ends.

The psalmist prays,
You gave me a wide place for my steps under me,
    and my feet did not slip.

And on a summer day in 1974,
I was driving my teenage car
        to the family graveyard
to copy tombstones
on a clear summer morning,

        when God assured me:
This prairie
where your kin lived
and are buried
is a wide place for all your days.

*

Near the prairie's end,

Grandma's granary fence
was patched with the door
of a '37 Chevy, lazy repair job and
my imagined gateway to childhood science:

the seas of Darwin,
        the peaks of Humboldt
and journeys of Wallace.
The smell of flowers on old walking clothes
makes the best day.

Fond branches of white ash,
honeysuckle brush,
its bell-shaped corolla, creeping growth,

pumpkins, gourds, strawberries,
her garden, her sickle
        a crescent moon,

always her African violets.

In winter, snow grew in the pastures,
and the Christmas carols
        returned from the off-season
brightened
        the day's dull heavens
                across the singing bridge….

She went like Elijah one night,

and for fifty years
the place of the farmhouse
        goes deep

into the hill.

I would push open the car door
        once more,

gather Earth's plants
tied with infinite ribbons,
return, and place them here.

*

Four Mile in the seasons,

an autumn photo in my office,

    names remembered
        from 19th century plat books
as I dream the roadside trees
and the fields:

Washburn, Severns, Pilcher, Fink,
        Kistler, Lichtenwalter, Griffith, Rush,
Mahon, Dr. Morey, Crawford, Sidwell, Rine;

    the names of other folks.

    I recite them
with my drive

when autumn paints colors,

when the timber turns cold and thistle-brown,

and when the green comes home.

*

Red clay of the timber soil,
the prairie's gray loam.
  The tangled bank,
which I cannot move through
with my two legs,
and a sickle without touching me
would draw my own blood.

God is the place of the world—
  so teaches a midrash—
but is contained by nothing

,

  as Jacob awakened
from his frightening dream of climbing seraphim
in a common place,
rocks and plants,
  where he found a way to Heaven.

Some have called these thin places,
  where what is most real
isn't so far from what we think we know
  for sure,

energy, insight, troubling,
  whatever your vision may be.

On Four Mile, Dad said one day,
I love how you can always see timber
in the distance on these old roads

  and eight years old,
I knew *the fountain-light of all our day.*

*

Crop rows stroll toward timber,
round bales seem to grow
        as plants of their own genus,

and down the way,
pumpjack wells
are steel grasshoppers rocking up and down,

with each stroke twenty liters of oil
drawn from sandstone pools
        of Pennsylvanian age
along anticlines of this Illinois basin.

The three branches of Sand Run
        flow here, toward the river
by flowing toward Hickory Creek,
                and Overcup Creek in the south.

        As a boy I got the notion
to hike the banks all the way to the Okaw
into which these waters empty,

but I only got as far as the sixty acres
by the country lane
        that only farmers use
to get their tractors to the fields
        by what I call the dirt cliff
where the land drops off twenty or thirty feet.

If I could paint in Hudson River style
all the Four Mile places,
the flowers, fields, and butterflies,

Sand Creek would be Kaaterskill Falls
and on the high land

I'd meet and chat
with dead relatives of my choice,
penciled in for repeatable increments
of sweet communion.

*

Four Mile is where I learned to drive,
              a perfect, quiet road on which
to make mistakes safely—
          my old '63 Chevy,
no AC, stick, AM adequate, hole
              in the driver's side floorboard,

Dad in the passenger seat,
          a truck driver who knew driving.

          You let the clutch out too quickly again.
          Never ride the clutch, you'll burn it out.
          Never ride the brakes, either.
          Always look over your shoulder when you pass.
          I TOLD YOU NOT TO LET THE CLUTCH OUT
          TOO QUICKLY!

Later, he bought me a newer car.
              In the meantime,
I drove the Chevy all over, with girlfriends,
buddies, library books, to class—
          and barefoot to Four Mile
for genealogy.

              Don't we miss our teenage cars!
when we gain that special freedom
          to drive
                  which, once acquired,
mastered, then taken for granted,
          never again
seems quite so sweet.

*

My mom's aunt and uncle
     lived down this side road.

She spent weekend nights there
          during Depression days
    for fun
and respite from farm drudgery,

riding their horse
    upon the country lane
toward Wilberton Township.

    And Mom's best friend
         lived by this other way,
neighbors, so they could walk to school
    together

and together they stayed, friends
    for eighty years.

Surely the troubles of old age
        could even be cherished

    if you had a friendship
older than many people live.

*

The Four Mile country store:
canned goods, cereal,
        auto repair products;
                famed lunch meat;
Carl the friendly owner—
                distant cousin—
        opened early and
stayed late for the farmers, the families and kids
        who came and went all the time—

for the "loafers," too,
solving the world's issues
        to their satisfaction.

Carl's family helped at the store.

Grapette, 76, and Orange Crush
stayed cold in redeemable bottles
        in the cooler
of fading Coke red.
I drank that orange right down
like TV cowboys took their whiskey,
        eliciting Mom's moral caution.

If I could go back in time, I'd find more bottle caps
strewn through the store's gravel parking lot
        beside Mom and Dad's car
and fill my pockets,

and then head off to other tasks,
        my pockets jingling.

*

I regret now that I was never here
on Sunday morning to attend a service
          of the Four Mile Prairie Christian Church,

founded 1843,
the pretty white building, with its
          Sunday school wing.

          Its first preacher is buried
in the family graveyard, and two
          of the first members.

Grandma and her quilters met here,
the "cheery do-a-lots."
          She made me a quilt,
fine patterns in remnants
          saved during years of sad widowhood
sewn onto the cream top
          and now kept precious
          in my cedar chest

away from sunlight, cat spit-up,
          spilled coffee,
                    and other natural enemies

of sacred cloth.

*

Someone needs to know
where you're from
          and whether so-and-so
is your kin. They're such good folks,
          and you must be, too.

There was once
          a party line for everyone.
Catch up on local news
if you were curious
          and remembered not to cough.

Now, I think of the wires stretching
among the farmhouses
on the state road and country roads;

          and the thin phone book
kept in a drawer for safe keeping
filled with names
of neighbors and
          with doodles on the cover.

Rural Route,
          the metal mailboxes
waiting for the man
to kick up gravel dust,
announce with his muffler
          that something may have arrived
for you,
          the creak of the lid,

          catalogues, fliers with coupons,
a handwritten letter from someone—
          even someone who just lives
down the road a bit.

Don't throw those letters out!
        Save them
for someone to love decades later.

I've a letter from my grandfather
        to his sister, writing about
how sick he felt. Of course, no one knew
        he'd die three weeks later...

One summer Grandma wrote me how
she'd killed a black snake with a hoe,

and caught a possum tail
in a trap she set for groundhogs
        and kept it in her freezer to show guests,
so proud.

*

She gave me a Bible dictionary,
a present for a boy
            sort of interested,
sort of not....

            But wait! *When the student is ready*
the books are at hand!
The books and their givers
                led you here! Teachers,
cherished friends appear,
                crisscross journeys
over millstones for walking,
                and the clock tower's gold.

Autumn leaves from home mark the pages.

            Where in the Book
are the cities of refuge,
                the descendants of the tribes,
clothing styles, empires,
            any name cross-referenced?

Maps—
Galilee's up,
            and Judea is down—
the journeys of Paul,
            rewinding the tables of the nations.

Back here, likely every house along this road
and all the side roads
            has a Bible,
the church has a shelf of them,
            a tabernacle of kindness and detail,
carried and enjoyed for your lifetime.

Add names and dates of family
in the front section
       and there you are in the very Good Book
with parents and uncles and aunts
and folks who died too young,

       who sit with the orchestra
in salvation history.

*

Down the way, there was once
        Noah's Ark Church,
that likely few remember now,
        for my uncle told me,
and he wasn't sure where it was, exactly,
        nor the denomination.

Someone cleared out the lumber,
took the concrete steps away
        and all the hymns.

For many years I drove by
        the old Mahon School
where Mom attended,
        her McGuffey Reader days,

and still drive by
though its timber, boards
        return to soil....

Nothing is holy apart from God,
                neither summer
nor all the seasons
nor the rocks and plants and animals.
Let me be Native so I can honor the spirits
        of each place I experience,

spirits and powers and weather and stories,
        mutuality and balance,
a holiness lodged in the very fibers.

But my ancestors gave Natives whiskey
and drove them beyond the far timber edges,
then wrote of them as if they were foolish.

I won't look for a thin place for an altar,

I'll tell you stories.

II

Decoration Day

*

      I layer Four Mile with names
long-lived in country histories
      of quarto size.

Where was the first house?
      John Wakefield—
local statesman, author of a book
            on the Black Hawk War
      in which he served—
built that house in the big election year of 1824,
      unending commotions
at the state capital, six miles west.

I dream the way
      this prairie might have looked back then,
first trees, grass that grew
above a person's head
      and might go to flames like nothing.

The same sun that burned the skin
      of ancestors rises above the cultivated fields.
      The same stars charted
pathways for runaway slaves

The same moon moves in its safe place
among the stars, a fair epic
in the brightening blue.

A sliver of hand-cut rail in the field,
a shard of baked jar,
an arrowhead of the Kickapoo
      driven out in tragedy;

clouds of unknowing
like a scratched daguerreotype.

Yes, if a tree falls in the woods,
it makes sound waves. But if a tree is cut down
to become a house in the woods,
you know it when a name is passed into writing,
    and these are the families.

It's the end of May,
    bouquets and flags to place....

*

3rd-great-grandfather David,
at the timber boundary
of our little graveyard
        with your consort Esther,

may we meet on Judgment Day
        with notions of the *Mayflower*
and our ancestors' survival
                that first winter
        chronicled by Bradford;

King Philip's tragic war;

and back to the churches of Plymouth,
        Leiden, Vrouwekerk,

and further yet, to Evesham's Norman gateway
as we walk the Avon Bridge
        to family graves,

even the swallow's music
        at the church of Wichenford

echoing to Four Mile
from Plantagenet England.

*

Family stories,
        told in carbon copies.

Robert dated a Catholic girl
who wouldn't see him during Lent, and he said,
        And by gosh, I respected her for it.

Cousin Lottie dyed her dress with strong coffee
        so it would be pretty
and cream-colored for church.

Great-great-grandmother Rhoda
always planted her cabbage seeds
        on St. Patrick's Day,
even if she had to plant them in the snow....

        The spooked horse upended
the wheat drill so that Andy fell hard
into the lever,

        and family gathered
in the bitter bedroom,
        waiting for the end
while beyond the window,
these boundaries of timber
for fields yearly tilled,

        and no bird ceased its song.

*

Does a rock mark
        the grave of the free woman
who came with our family
from Kentucky to care
for their children
        as rough Father plowed
and Mother sewed?

Perhaps she is a story,
        a tired anecdote
of loyal and happy nanny slaves.
Perhaps she's true, and
        this was her choice
for security within a modicum of freedom.

If so, with children she watched and fed,
she is safe
        in beautiful Zion

while we march for her.

*

Abe's profile graces
      Heritage Trail signs
            where this road continues up
to Hillsboro;
      he names license plates
          of Illinois; and
drug store postcards four score and ten.

Is it too much to say
      that Illinois wildflowers
          and stones cry out
with malice toward none?

      What lovely grace
that Winslow Pilcher—
      War of 1812 vet,
husband of Averilla, matriarch—
hauled timber
to the Vandalia public square
          for use in the new statehouse
     in 1836,

and so, young Lincoln
had a place to serve,
and we hometown folks could be
      always boast of our heritage.

      I remember when taps
were played in 1972,
when Winslow's grave
      had his name at last.

*

4th-great-grandfather Thomas,
    of an old Virginia family,
Died Sept. 11, 1856, Aged about 71 Years.

There was an Independence Day barbeque
    here on the prairie in 1837

with the reading of the Declaration
    and toasts all around.
Thomas toasted his blessings:
57 years have seen me a free man
    and 99 x 57 will still see me free,
not a slave to a tyrant.

    On the 145th anniversary
of his death, my wife was in Manhattan
    and saw the second tower fall.

I place my own American memories
    upon his grave.

*

Jesus said suffer the children
and forbid them not
for such is the Kingdom of Heaven

      like Cyrene, Ulysses, Lucy Jane,
Alonzo

The Rose may fade, the body die
but Flowers unmarked bloom on high.

Julie, Emma,

      infant 6 days, infant 9 days,

        ITW
          A

Eudoxy rests here,
and Roselma, Ira, Mortimore,
young Walter Rush.
      Our darling one hath gone before
      to greet us on the blissful shore.

Theredore, Alphesis…

Edney and Adney were
      unusually pretty babies,
said Grandma.

Elvina and Lemuel
      lie in the far corner,
          a warning,
for they had smallpox.

      Beyond the land of sinful powers

our child is safe in Eden's bowers.

Remember all these beloved,
who breathed so briefly, if at all.

*

Great-great-grandpa was at "Verry Cruz"
when his mother died, 1847,
waiting for letters from him
      though none came in time.

Telegraphy was new,
unused to alert a prairie settler
where her armed boy was.

Scott's forces, amphibious
landing without a shot,
      then the siege, and Cerro Gordo
toward Alta California and
Santa Fe de Nuevo México,
      belated recognition of Texas.

northern territories lost, cities,
Mexican shame and assessment,
fresh honor for the dead
      at Chapultepec Park.

Each Memorial Day,
we visit mother and son,
her effigy slab, his stone ever
brightened with drug store flags.
      Perchance he dreams
of Boca del Río.

*

Blacksmith Moses
had a finely carved stone

but it is broken. These sixty years
I've seen it sink
            into the soil,

fallen backward. His name
can be seen in the sun,

so there's that.

But as a boy, how I loved
            his strange grave,
the death date larger than the arched name,
the *memento mori* epitaph,

awakening a wanderlust for
            history,
                        thank you, Moses…

I imagine
he played a fiddle at his forge
in the firefly evening:
            old-time tunes for country dancing,
maybe Mozart, Boccherini,

and the music still flows through every leaf,
            every needle of the spruce

to this day.

*

Old books have home remedies.
Guinea peppers, their reddish berries
       warmth for the stomach,
excitement for languid organs.

Dried foxglove leaves
twice a day may be good for dropsy,
but avoid the chrysanthemum
       and its alarming symptoms.

Great-great-grandfather had his laudanum
       instead, delirious
from his dropsy, calling out

       though his kids were already there.
His obelisk in the graveyard
is a little
       axis mundi
beside the pasture fence

       and I regain
my sense of direction.

*

Uncle Charlie Pilcher
lived down the road
        at the curb into the timber.

He waved at the drivers on the road,
        the wagons and the cars.
There he passed away on his porch
in farm quiet
                by his lilacs.

He had a sister who was so tiny
        as a baby,
they say you could've put a teacup
on her head
        and it would rest on her shoulders.
She lived down the way, too,
                a little farther.

He always went to hear Old Ben Mahon preach
        at Meeting
and he always come forward to have his foot washed.

        How I wish I could say
I saw his spirit
giving me greeting on the road
before he returns to his far corner,

        spruce needles a casket spray.

*

A farmer filled his empty oatmeal box
with papers.

I dump them on my bed:
        a Sunday school program for 1905—
The Slavs in America—
hospital bills for his sick wife,
a slip of paper with the address
        at a St Louis hotel
for his prodigal brother.

        A church lesson:
O friend, this Holy Book will long last
beyond this twentieth century:
Let us love it
and read it
and live by God's light.

        A folded poster
for their farm sale:
thirteen head of hogs, horses and cows
and implements of all kinds,
20 acres of corn, still in the field,
        money to raise for a dying son…

Their house still stands,
        once Advent blue,
not far from here.

*

Auntie got eye strain,
the stereoscope pressed against her face
     so often,
each image to each eye and then blending,
that addictive
illusion of depth and dimension.

It's not that she didn't love the farm,
     nor did she long for more of the world
than what she'd seen
and what would have saved to see.

But she fancied traveling the globe
     as a stereographer, visiting place after place
from Lincoln's home
to the Taj Mahal to the Cliffs of Dover

and any place or sight worthy
of a dream's double image.

*

Grandpa found 78 morels beneath a tree!
Where? When?

So long ago,
        1910s,
when he walked wide-eyed
over black, sandy soil
in the chilly light
        of the farm's far side,

awaiting the homely vision.

        There are places
where you had luck one year
but not the next,

        and places
where you stood astonished
beside the fallen trees,

God's earthy gladness,
        the flavor of place.

*

Cousin Louis was in France—
over there, over there—
hopeful to see the Holy Land
     after his service…

dying in the base hospital at St. Naziarre,
          a fortnight before Passchendaele
while Ottoman and British trenches
stretched across the Negev
from Gaza
     to Beersheba.

I will follow Thee my Saviour,
Whereso'er my lot shall be.

He led you
from the slaughter,
          honored son.

Great-grandfather Albert
built Grandma's house,
      and I love to walk into rooms
      that have not existed
for fifty years;
      the never locked porch leading
to the kitchen, with its pump for cistern water,
      the pantry to the side, her aprons
hanging over farm calendars;

      the warm living room
where I pause to nap, warm and happy
      on the sofa near the coal burning stove
and the dark desk to the side.

I peak into the bedroom with its stale,
magical wardrobe,
      the delicate figurines—
blue birds, ladies in gowns—
and the front room,

      where I sit and leaf
through her magazines:
Bible study quarterlies,
      Look and *Life* magazines.
Yes, here is that issue
with Veruschka, so pretty.

      I go out the side door,
stand on the board step
      and gaze at the layers
of spruce needles
nourishing the mowed grass.

I walk around the back
and stroll the dense back acres
where the ground slopes
            then rises to the little
hilltop, with trees
        I feared to climb

and would not dare to, now,
but they are here, for the robins, doves
        in an overgrown place.

       I breathe in nature
and it breathes back.
             The grass and I remember.

*

Jacob Mahon
      was brother of
            Harriet and Caroline
and they married Crawford brothers Calvin and Andrew
                    while Jacob married Rosetta Bolt
      but Harriet died
            leaving Calvin widowed
and Jacob died
            leaving Rosetta widowed
then Rosetta married Calvin,
      and Andrew
had long since died
            then Caroline
      married Bill Smail,

and that's why you devote some time
      when you chat with a genealogist.

*

Seven Crawford siblings
        are buried in a line
in order of their age.

                Was that planned?
            Surely not,
but I thought it was cool.

        They traveled to this township
with their widowed mother
from Ohio along the National Road,
        remembering their father,
            buried in Waldo

            (where is Waldo?) north
                of Columbus.

*

Ben Mahon,
Irish grandson,
Old School Baptist preacher,
    Avena Twp. farmer.

    May the road rise up to meet you,
    may the wind be always at your back...

He preached 100 to 150 sermons a year,
            never taking any money,
till he was buried here in shade
    with his wife and young daughters.

In my imagination,
        he rode west toward Vandalia
and southeast toward St. Peter
        and to Overcup and Avena and all over,

and he knew his Bible.
        Jeroboam to Hoshea,
        Rehoboam to Zedekiah,
all those kings of Israel and Judah in order
        and backward,
and the tribes of Israel
        and where they settled both sides
of the Jordan
and the way the Tabernacle looked
        and how Ezekiel's Temple looked,
and even how the End Times would be
        all laid out.

as he read the scriptures beneath the big tree
        in Mr. Pilcher's graveyard
where Preacher Chaffin of Four Mile

was buried
            long before.

Good and faithful servants.

*

I dream
        a sermon:

        Enjoy your evening, beloved,
beneath these trees
that border Four Mile,

for God rescues with trees,

Noah's gopher wood,
the shittim wood of the Ark,
the Temple's Lebanon cedar,

the Cross:
stationary wheel
with Life at its center.

The Bible bookends
with the Tree of Life,
        the great shade of Eden
the plentitude of water of life
that flows from the throne of God,
        bright as crystal
and waters the tree of life,
        its leaves for the healing of the nations.

The soul is perennial,
emerging nourished
through dryness and storms
        by the water of life.

The soul is annual,
planted new for each place,

God's mysterious horticulture,
selections and rejections,
fig withered though out of season

    unexpected plant grafts
take, impossibly…

    Cherish the Scriptures, beloved,

sun and stars for Torah,
flowers and rain for Prophets,
singing birds for Psalms and Writings,
    pleasant breeze and trees
for Gospels and Letters,
storm and rainbow for Revelation,
    a truthful road that is the Way;

    and throughout,
the march
    of Egypt, Assyria, Babylon, Persia,
Greece, and Rome,

    but God does not esteem
what we call power, what we call greatness.

Even the nations are like a drop from a bucket,
and are accounted as dust on the scales.

No, God opens his heart to all who turn to him,
    more than we could ask or think.

God opens his heart to you,
    and nothing you could do
will close it.

    Nothing.

He will not let your foot be moved;
he who keeps you will not slumber.

He who keeps Israel
   will neither slumber nor sleep.

This evening, beloved,
know that through sundry and traveled places
          the Good Book unfurls
along worn paths
                    like our very road:

Samaria, Shechem, Shittim,
          Hebron, Jezreel, Jerusalem,
Christ's ways of sorrow.

The Great Trunk Road:
          from Egypt to Megiddo,
and to the seaside toward Antioch.

          Remember how the Israelites
so long before,
hungry and bitter, deplored the roads,

          for Sinai had no wealth like the cities.
                    Like us, they couldn't behave,
they felt afraid.

But those gathered people gained
          their precious direction
in a homesick place,

and thereby they knew God accompanied them
everywhere and anywhere.

          Mary and Joseph knew it
so long later,
as they carried their baby Jesus to Egypt
on the Way of the Sea.
The people gained their precious commandments
in a homesick place

and by this we know
that any place is the place to serve Jesus
with our good deeds
    and words of Life.

Enjoy your evening, beloved,
        on this land that your mothers and fathers
gained through treaties,
claimed for their own
    struggled to gain, to buy,
your own place for a season,
yet not your own,

for the earth is the Lord's
    and all things therein,

and all things work together in God's wisdom.

A voice cries from the highway,

The Lord is the everlasting God,
  the Creator of the ends of the earth.

    God gave the people Canaan
because Eden had been lost,

    and so Canaan became their Eden,
and they settled with Judah in the south
and tribes in between,
Asher and Nephtali in the north
and the tribes across the river,
    and yet do not hold tight
to anything that passes away.
            A voice cries,
All people are grass,
  their constancy is like the flower of the field.
but the word of our God will stand for ever.

Remember this
    as you sojourn
in this home place
    and see the spring butterflies
    announce the Resurrection,

the cabbage white and swallowtail,
blue azure and the question mark:

God cares for the land and the waters,
    and the deer and the rabbit and
all creatures here below.

God remembers his people.

God dwells among his people.

He dries every tear.

He joins in our laughter.

He remembers the Jordan,

where our souls wait in eager anticipation
    to cross over

to beautiful, beautiful Zion....

III

Rural Route

*

Power lines above the trees
draping to the next tower,

the road at peace,

and still another memory appears:
1960, our gold Cadillac,
        back seat pillows and fried chicken
warm in foil,

        my View-Master™ for
seeing the world,

a coffee can to catch my pee and later
to water the ditch lilies.

Eye blink and a lump in the throat
and that trip to Tennessee
        that began at Four Mile
is so long ago

        savored like the sight
of a Rock City barn on Route 51.

Why relive what's past?
Why not? I might die before …
I finish … this line…

        Whew, still safe! to love yesterday
at the sight of a leaf, a road,
        a day by the culvert water.

*

Woodwind chords fall
like a gentle rain through timber,
leaves dripping water in the flutes;

     choirs of cathedrals
and the scripture promises.

No place is more dear
     than the one
your favorite music sets.

There's rain today
as I sit at home,
     and somewhere in the timber
the place of the farm pond
may still have cattails
     dragonflies and their nymphs
in the fresh water,
     a perfect theme in pentatonic scale
and the rumble of timpani thunder.

*

Faith, hope, and love,
       these three,
and how great is a place
            where they took root in you,

where God knit cloths
       of yourself
that you recognize

in the scenes
       and the road
and the houses and the clouds,

       and each bird for your visit,
its feathers drab or bright.

*

Four Mile is the dove
that first taught me the word *melancholy,*
    hoo-hooing grayly along
the tangled brush of the fence row,

and the spot in the forest
    where Kickapoo hunters
danced into the night
    as the insects and birds
cried their own chorus,

and the field where three 1800s children
    were buried in a corner
once fenced off,

and the grave of the boy who fought at Vicksburg
    and heard the bugler play the seventh,

and the fence of the old agronomy station
    with its pump that poured cool water,

and the roadside tree that stopped a car,
    the wounded bark healed over
as if by the touch of Christ

who comforts all who mourn.

*

Four Mile is the robin
who greets Otego Township,
        St. James, and Loogootee;

who grants orange beauty
to the new clematis
that hugs the winter firewood
        beyond the hostas;

who lights upon the propane tank
and the milk house filled with magazines
        and the children's swing
set up in the back;

who loves the place of Duck Curry's
                antiques store,
his flow blue and carnival glass
        and postcards
and cherished furniture;

who knows the killdeer
that nests with worry
in the church's gravel parking lot;

who knows the chewing cows
that gaze at you in contentment
        from beyond the fence;

who knows the searching gyres
        of the dark birds,
homely neighbors who cannot sing;

who traces bean rows
        planted surely across the land;

who preaches Resurrection.

*

Four Mile is the blue jay
who flies from Brownstown

where the Vandalia Railroad
once carried folks over to the St. Louis World's Fair
        to see Japan, Jerusalem,
and all the pavilions;

where Sam Wead's store and the Stine store
and the Rode store and D.O. Pilcher's store
        and Griffith Bros. & Co.
and Bingaman & Son
        opened on time for business;

where folks went up to McCoy's for lunch
        and O'Dell's for wheel repair,
and over to Vandalia—

the jay that visits the homes once owned by folks
        who turned down Jack Benny on the radio,
even Jack Benny, to talk about
        the coming elections;

and the homes with their TVs
        that reported JFK and MLK,
Vietnam, 9/11, Covid;

and homes where little kids like me
breached mashed potato dams,
        of turkey gravy,
wiping out the green beans;

and the barns filled with straw
and sure tools handy;

and the tractors and combines
       that the farmers keep running
from morning deep into evening;

and the jay's noisy call
       alerts others of the presence
of the hawk.

*

Four Mile is the cardinal,
        beautiful male and female
who call out,
Peace be with you, be not afraid,

who visit folks in sight of their riding mowers
and perch upon wire fences
        and IDOT signs

and mailboxes set straight in roadside soil;

who travel the country lanes
        where bobwhite burst
into startled flight;

who gladdens the yards
where kinfolk visit on warm days
        before going inside for coffee
or iced tea and ginger cookies,

        and where the deer
stroll up in twilight
        to eat your roses;

who remind folks
that Saturday is the next trip
        over to St. Louis
to see a ball game.

*

I travel my hands' secret heartline:

up the slight hill
        past the young girl's grave;
that road's gray, humble width
        laid in 1920s specs;
and then a few minutes' drive

until I reach the curve into timber
near the Brownstown Road
        and this prairie ends.

        How precious the day
when I was driving my teenage car
        to the family graveyard
to copy tombstones
on a clear summer morning

and God assured me:
This prairie
where your kin lived
and are buried
is a wide place for all your days.

*

The Lord will keep you from all evil;
  he will keep your life.
The Lord will keep
  your going out and your coming in
  from this time on and for evermore.

What may your last thoughts be,
as you pass from world to World
and rise to Life

as surely as pillars of fire
shine over water?

May God share your prayers
with topography,
the love that became
      your fountain-light

for all your days

as companion angels say,

            Welcome home.

Notes and Acknowledgements

I have never lived at Four Mile Prairie. These poems are those of someone who has visited the place for over sixty years.

"How beautiful a highway…" Illinois state route 185 is the highway of these poems. It was the last of the original Illinois state routes established in 1918 and 1924. At that time, it extended 20 miles from Bluff City to Farina. Now, it also goes through Vandalia and northwest to Hillsboro.

The last lines echo a famous quotation by Katherine Mansfield, found on numerous sites of inspiring statements: "How hard it is to escape from places. However carefully one goes they hold you - you leave little bits of yourself fluttering on the fences - like rags and shreds of your very life."

"Sheltering…" *You gave me a wide place* is Psalm 18:36.

"Red clay…" The midrash *God is the place of the world…* is from Genesis Rabbah 68:9. … *the fountain-light of all our day* is from Wordsworth's "Ode: Intimations of Immortality."

"Crop rows…" incorporates portions of "Pump Jacks," from my chapbook *Little River* (Georgetown, KY: Finishing Line Press, 2017). The name Kaaterskill Falls alludes to the painting *Kindred Spirits* by Asher Brown Durand.

"The Four Mile country store…" In addition to my own memories, I appreciate Panzi Blackwell's article, "Looking back to the days of the Four Mile Store," *The Leader-Union* (Vandalia, IL), January 12, 1996.

"I regret now…" incorporations a portion of "Grandma's Quilt" from my chapbook, *Dreaming at the Electric Hobo* (Georgetown, KY: Finishing Line Press, 2015). The poem first appeared in *Tantra Press*.

"Down the way, there was once…" Yi-Fu Tuan discusses how, in Native American spirituality, all things are in some sense living. Narrative of heroic persons as well as ritual bring landscapes to life. In Christianity, this sacredness of place, invigorated by narrative, are also present but to a lesser degree. Yi-Fu Tuan, with photographs and essays by Martha A. Strawn,

Religion: From Place to Placelessness (Chicago, The Center for American Places at Columbia College, 2009), 12-14.

"I layer Four Mile with names…" incorporates portions of "Settlement" from my chapbook, *Dreaming at the Electric Hobo*. The poem first appeared in *Big Muddy*. John A. Wakefield was the first white settler of the prairie (and my first cousin by marriage six times removed). Later, he wrote *A History of the War Between the United States and the Sac and Fox Nations of Indians…* Jacksonville: Calvin Goudy, 1834.

For poetic purposes I've conflated the Pilcher Cemetery and the nearby, smaller Winslow Pilcher Family Cemetery. Here are my 1974 transcriptions of graves in both cemeteries: paulstroble.files.wordpress. com/2016/11/scan-4.pdf and paulstroble.files.wordpress.com/2016/11/ scan-6.pdf.

"3rd great-grandfather David…" see https://paulstroble.wordpress.com/2017/06/01/the-washbourne-family-in-england/

"Family stories, told in carbon copies…" incorporates a portion of my poem "Scattering," first published in *Little River*. Several family stories are from the Winslow Pilcher family history written by my grandma's first cousin Blanche (Schwarm) Harstad. Carbon copies were given to family members.

"Abe's profile graces…" incorporates a portion of a poem from my collection, *Walking Lorton Bluff* (Georgetown, KY: Finishing Line Press, 2020).

"4th great-grandfather Thomas…" My ancestor Thomas R. Gatewood's July 4th toast was recorded in the *Illinois State Register*, July 22, 1837.

"Old books…" These remedies are from A. B. Strong, *The American Flora* (New York: Strong and Burdick, 1845).

"Auntie got eye strain…" is a slight revision of "Stereoscope," which appeared in *Little River*.

"Stereoscope" first appeared in *Pegasus* and won first place in the 2016 Adult Poetry contest of the Kentucky State Poetry Society. Unlike other poems in this sequence, this one is imaginary. But it was inspired my stereoscope with cards purchased from Millard "Duck" Curry's antique shop, a favorite family stop run by a family friend, just south of Four Mile's highway.

"Grandpa found 48 morels…" is a revision of "Morels," which appeared in my chapbook, *Small Corner of the Stars* (Georgetown, KY: Finishing Line Press, 2017).

"Cousin Louis was in France—" The quotation *I will follow Thee my Saviour, Wheresoe'er my lot shall be* is from Frederick M. Hanes, *Fayette County in the World War* (Vandalia: The Vandalia Union, 1922), 59. Louis Crawford (my first cousin three times removed) was the first local casualty in World War I. He is one of the namesakes of the Crawford-Hale American Legion Post #95 in Vandalia, established August 2, 1919. Coincidentally, that was the day my mother was born at the family home.

"Ben Mahon…." A biographical sketch for Benjamin Mahon (my 4th-great-uncle) appears in *History of Fayette County, Illinois* (Philadelphia: Brink, McDonough & Co., 1878), 91. Grandma, who was 12 when he died, remembered him.

"I dream a sermon…" This is not a sermon of Ben's (I don't know if any exist) but my own musings of spirituality and place, which I would share with my pioneer relatives for an evening homecoming. The scripture quotations are Psalm 121:3-4; Isaiah 40:6-8, 15, 28; Rev. 22:1-2.

The section "Woodwind chords…" as well as the line *heard the bugler play the seventh*, allude to Ralph Vaughan Williams' *A Pastoral Symphony*, a significant inspiration for these poems. As RVW honored the war dead through music suggesting landscape peace, I remember my grandmother Grace (Pilcher) Crawford through my personal experience of the landscape where she lived her whole life. The first months of pandemic quarantine in 2020 brought about the first draft of these poems, in about three weeks.

"Four Mile is the blue jay…" A few details among these poems came from the locally published *A Century of History of Brownstown, Illinois, 1870-1970* and *A 125th Year Celebration, Brownstown, Illinois, 1870-1995*.

"*The Lord will keep you from all evil…*" The quotation is Psalm 121:7-8. The rest of the poem echoes the first sentence of Annie Dillard, *An American*

Childhood (New York: Harper & Row, 1987).

The background of these poems can be found in essays on my blog, "Grace, Place, and the Like," https://paulstroble.wordpress.com, especially the trio of essays "The House and the Farm," "Thinking About History," and "Local People." Those essays originally appeared in my book *Journeys Home,* self-published in 1995 and 2000. That book collected several pieces that were first published in *Springhouse* magazine. Another background of these poems is the genealogical work that I did, while a high school student in the '70s. I traced the Crawford family history, transcribed the Pilcher Cemetery inscriptions (see above), and traced other families of Otego Township, of which Four Mile Prairie is a part, for the Fayette County Genealogical Society. Another background to these poems is my book, *You Gave Me a Wide Place: Holy Places of Our Lives* (Nashville: Upper Room Books, 2006), where I (and several of my friends) reflect on the spiritual significance of locations.

Many thanks to my family, Beth and Emily and all our cats; Dr. Tom Dukes, who encouraged this and previous projects and who made possible my dreams of writing poetry; poetry friends Kenneth Pruitt, Andrea Scarpino, Heathen, Jane Ellen Ibur; the Webster Groves Starbucks, the Novel Neighbor Bookstore, the St. Louis Poetry Center; and my dear friend Stacey Stachowicz and her family. These poems are dedicated to my grandma, my parents, and the numerous relatives and friends with whom I share connections to this prairie. I also remember friends Rev. Arthur C. and Marion Bryant, who are buried a few miles down the road at Loogootee—my next stop each time I visit Four Mile.

$\mathbf{P}$aul Stroble teaches philosophy and religious studies at Webster University in St. Louis and is also adjunct faculty at Eden Theological Seminary. A native of Vandalia, Illinois, he lives in St. Louis. A grantee of the National Endowment for the Humanities and the Louisville Institute, he has written several books, primarily church related, and numerous articles, essays, and curricular materials. Finishing Line Press has also published his collection *Walking Lorton Bluff* (2020) and the chapbooks *Dreaming at the Electric Hobo* (2015), *Little River* (2017), *Small Corner of the Stars* (2017), and *Backyard Darwin* (2019).

www.ingramcontent.com/pod-product-compliance
Lightning Source LLC
Chambersburg PA
CBHW021200090426
42740CB00008B/1172